PIANO ACCOMPANIMENTS/ ENSEMBLE SCORES

TEAM BRASS

RICHARD DUCKETT

The author is donating a percentage of his royalties from Team Brass
To the Save The Children Fund

TREVOR JONES
BRASS
& WOODWIND
7.95

International Music Publications

For MARY

Edited by WILLIAM RUMFORD Instrumental Organiser
for the London Borough of Brent
PHILIP EVRY and GEOFFRY RUSSELL-SMITH

Piano accompaniments by GEOFFRY RUSSELL-SMITH

INTERNATIONAL MUSIC PUBLICATIONS would like to thank the
following publishers for permission to use arrangements
of their copyright material in TEAM BRASS.
CHAPPELL MUSIC LTD. London W1Y 3FA
for LITTLE DONKEY
© 1959 Chappell Music Ltd.
WARNER BROS MUSIC LTD. London W1P 3DD
for BLOWIN' IN THE WIND
© 1962 (unpub.) © 1963 M Witmark & Sons, USA
and for STAR WARS (Main Title)
© 1977 Fox Fanfare Music Inc. USA
WILLIAMSON MUSIC LTD. London W1Y 3FA
for MY FAVORITE THINGS and EDELWEISS
© 1959 Richard Rodgers & Oscar Hammerstein II
Williamson Music Inc. USA

Sincere thanks are extended
to the following people whose criticism, advice
and help in various ways has been invaluable.
KEITH ALLEN, Senior Instrumental Teacher
for the City of Birmingham.
COLIN MOORE, County Instrumental Organiser
for East Sussex.
BRIAN WICKS, Senior Lecturer at Newman and Westhill
Colleges of Higher Education.
KEITH WATTS, Head of Brass for Sandwell Education Authority.
PETER SMALLEY, Cornet / trumpet player
and Instrumental Teacher, County of Staffordshire.
MOLLY WICKS and PHILIP LEAH, whose enthusiasm
and support have been a great encouragement.

First Published 1988
© Copyright International Music Publications

Exclusive Distributors
International Music Publications
Southend Road, Woodford Green,
Essex IG8 8HN

Book Design: Eleanor Gamper
Cover Design: Ian Barrett / Peter White
Cover Photography: Ron Goldby
Production: Peter White / Philip Evry
Reprographics: Positive Colour Ltd.
Instruments photographed by courtesy
of Vincent Bach International Ltd.

TEAM BRASS: Piano Accompaniments / Ensemble Scores
ISBN 0 86359 539 1 / Order Ref: 16699 / 215-2-433

Introducing Team Brass

The Individual Course

TEAM BRASS is structured to suit the requirements of all beginners, whatever their age or experience. New concepts are introduced singly and these are reinforced by Rhythm Grids or Letter Name Grids, for those who need them. As a general rule, the music at the top of each new 'concept page' is simpler than the music lower down the page and is particularly suitable for designing 'easy' courses for the youngest players. Courses which give more rapid progress can also be selected. For example, by proceeding via pages 3, 6, 8, 11, 12 and on to pages 22 and 23, the most able beginner can be playing an extended, fifty-bar accompanied solo — *Sleigh Ride* — within a few lessons.

The ensemble material also provides music of varying complexity within the same playing range. So whilst children of primary school age will cope easily with *German Tune* and *Lullaby* on page 14 for example, the *Canzonetta* on page 15 will appeal particularly to secondary aged students. Study options are provided at the foot of most pages so that the material can be used with great flexibility; the number of routes through TEAM BRASS is almost unlimited.

The Ensemble Course

TEAM BRASS ensemble music is drawn from Baroque, Classical, Folk, Hymns and Popular Song, and has been arranged to be playable by most combinations of instruments.

Whilst the extended ensemble material starts on page 14, many of the pieces from pages 2 to 11 also can be played together. Some of these offer the facility of combining B♭ and F instrumentalists. Pages 6 and 7 in all books fit together harmonically and rhythmically, and serve as a meeting point for pupils approaching from the upper or lower starting notes.

All TEAM BRASS ensemble pieces are carefully graded. A group of beginners therefore can learn to play exclusively from this material, should the need arise. Or lessons can be timetabled so that pupils meet as a group every second or third week, perhaps alternating with individual or smaller group lessons. Some of the ensemble pieces are songs which will be known to many children. This allows for a group of brass players to be integrated into a classroom music session, which might also include some percussion/keyboard accompaniment, as well as voices.

GCSE Music Skills

Although some instrumental teachers are prepared to help GCSE students with composing, listening and improvisation, research has shown that these skills should be introduced to *all* children as early as possible, before inhibitions are acquired which hinder the natural creative processes. TEAM BRASS provides material designed to help beginners develop their creative abilities during the lesson and at home.

Play by Ear Lines:

If pupils have been encouraged, for example, to repeat short phrases played by the teacher (or another pupil) in lessons, then the PLAY BY EAR lines are a useful aid for further instrument related aural practice. More experienced students might be encouraged to notate their results, possibly transposing the extracts into different keys.

Rhythm Grids:

Some children are happy to improvise and compose 'freely'; others find a rhythmical framework helpful in the early stages. At first a grid can simply be played through, using scale patterns. Then pupils can be encouraged to use more complex shapes. Of course, Rhythm Grids are only an aid, and children are happiest when composing a piece which conveys a specific mood or subject like 'sadness', 'sleigh-ride', 'Autumn'; or setting words, as in Joanne O'Neill's piece on page 22. As a transitional stage pupils can be encouraged to make up their own Rhythm Grids. Eventually they will be able to do without them completely.

The Quadratone:

Improvisation can be simplified in the early stages by using a 'restricted scale' based upon an easy fingering. One such device used in TEAM BRASS (on pages 6, 7, 17, 36, 43 and 48) is based upon the notes C, E, G and A, using just the 'open' instrument and first and second valves. As well as being suited to compositional scenarios like 'lullaby' and 'fanfare', the Quadratone can be used for early jazz improvisation over an adapted twelve-bar blues sequence in B flat:

4 x Bars B♭; 2 x Bars E♭; 2 x Bars B♭; 2 x Bars E♭; 2 x Bars B♭.

A more complex jazz scale based on the notes C, E♭, F, G, A♭, and B♭ and all played 'open', first valve, and second and third valves, (over the accompanying chords of B♭ minor 7 and E♭ minor 7) can follow on from this. This scale is used in TEAM BRASS in *The Swinger* on page 46. At later stages students can be helped to create their own scale variants.

Pre-literate Activities

It is important to let beginners experiment with an instrument before learning to read music. Using the mouthpiece in order to imitate noises like American Police sirens, ambulances, seagulls etc., encourages effective embouchure development and is a good starting point for handling and talking about sound in a sensitive way. Likewise, the instrument's creative and musical versatility can be explored by using mouthpiece, water-keys, slides, singing into the instrument, etc., to make sound effects like creaking doors, bells and 'howls' etc. These various sound effects can be used by several players to make a complete soundscape, or to tell a musical story, similar to the ones children will be used to creating in class music sessions. If there is a continual encouragement of these experiments while the child is acquiring music literacy, then the foundation will have been laid for the development of real compositional skills.

Profiling:

In order that the diverse aspects in each pupil's musical development can be organised into a 'structured whole', an example Assessment Profile is printed below.

Half-termly Profile

YEAR: _____   TERM: _____

NAME: _____   CLASS: _____

INSTRUMENT: _____

ASSESS THE STUDENT'S ABILITY TO:—

	Manages extremely well	Manages fairly well	Experiences some difficulty	Experiences much difficulty
Listen sensitively and critically:				
Read music:				
Acquire new techniques on the instrument:				
Interpret music imaginatively:				
Play 'by ear' (Listening Games etc.):				
Improvise:				
Express ideas, emotions (etc.) through composing:				
Notate sounds accurately:				
Contribute positively to group music sessions (Band etc.):				
Show originality in ideas for composition/improvisation:				
Take the initiative over new repertoire:				

Ensemble Scores

The scores provide a general guide to the TEAM BRASS ensemble material. However some instrumental combinations include parts which, for musical or technical reasons, will be found to differ occasionally from those printed below.

Harmony long notes
Pupil's page 19

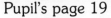

Unison long notes
Pupil's page 19

Slurred slow notes
Pupil's page 19

Slurred fast notes
Pupil's page 19

Regal fanfare
Pupil's page 20

When I first came to this land
Pupil's page 20

Traditional

Fast and furious

Blowin' in the wind
Pupil's page 21

Words and Music by
BOB DYLAN

Steadily

Chorus

Au claire de la lune
Pupil's page 37

Traditional

D.C. al Fine

Fine

Little donkey
Pupil's page 37

Words and Music by
ERIC BOSWELL

Harmony long notes
Pupil's page 38

Unison long notes
Pupil's page 38

Scale exercise
Pupil's page 38

Slurs
Pupil's page 38

Tijuana brass
Pupil's page 39

Brightly

I saw three ships
Pupil's page 39

Traditional

Happily

Michael row the boat
Pupil's page 48

Traditional

Canzona
Pupil's page 48

ADRIANO BANCHIERI
(1568-1634)

Allegro

O Little Town of Bethlehem

Pupil's page 49

Traditional

St. Anthony chorale

Pupil's page 49

JOSEPH HAYDN
(1732-1809)

March

Pupil's page 55

GEORGE FRIDERIC HANDEL
(1685-1759)

Piano Accompaniments

Contents

Pavane and Elegy

Pupil's pages 3 and 5

Acapulco Bay

Pupil's pages 6 and 7

Tempo di Beguine

Watch Your Step!

Pupil's page 8

Vigorous March

Les Ballons

Pupil's page 13

Daniel Ryan →

Sleigh Ride Louise Barrett
Pupil's page 23

Allegro Moderato

f sempre leggiero

loud

sim.

* N.B. These repeated bars are written out in full in the instrumental copy

Victorian Ballad

Pupil's page 26

* 2nd time to Coda

* The two-bar Coda appears only in the piano copy.

My Favourite Things

Pupil's page 31

Words by OSCAR HAMMERSTEIN II
Music by RICHARD RODGERS

Edelweiss

Pupil's page 35

Words by OSCAR HAMMERSTEIN II
Music by RICHARD RODGERS

Semplice

Ben con ped.

Theme from Polovtsian Dances

Pupil's page 36

ALEXANDER BORODIN (1833-87)

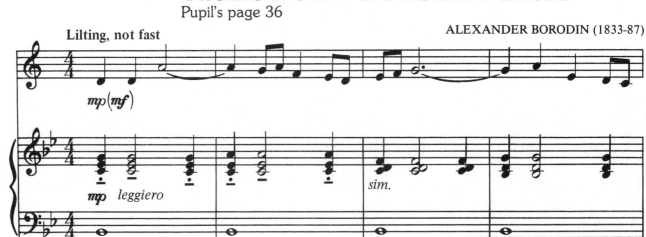

Scottish Ballad

Pupil's page 43

Caribbean Dance

Pupil's page 44

Traditional

The Centipede's Masterpiece

Pupil's page: B♭ 52, Tbn. 𝄢 57

SARAH HART

'Star Wars' Main Title

Pupil's page: B♭ 56, Tbn. 𝄢 60

JOHN WILLIAMS

March
Pupil's page 57

GEORGE FRIDERIC HANDEL (1685-1759)

Pavane and Elegy

Pupil's pages 3 and 5

Acapulco Bay

Pupil's pages 6 and 7

Watch Your Step!

Pupil's page 8

Les Ballons

Pupil's page 13

Sleigh Ride
Pupil's page 23

Allegro Moderato

loud

mf sempre leggiero

f

1*

2

* N.B. These repeated bars are written out in full in the instrumental copy

Victorian Ballad

Pupil's page 26

In relaxed style

* 2nd time to Coda

* The two-bar Coda appears only in the piano copy.

My Favourite Things

Pupil's page 31

Words by OSCAR HAMMERSTEIN II
Music by RICHARD RODGERS

Edelweiss

Pupil's page 35

Words by OSCAR HAMMERSTEIN II
Music by RICHARD RODGERS

Theme from Polovtsian Dances

Pupil's page 36

ALEXANDER BORODIN (1833-87)

Scottish Ballad

Pupil's page 43

Caribbean Dance

Pupil's page 44

Traditional

The Centipede's Masterpiece

Pupil's page 52

SARAH HART

'Star Wars' Main Title

Pupil's page 56

JOHN WILLIAMS

March

Pupil's page 57

GEORGE FRIDERIC HANDEL (1685-1759)

Pavane and Elegy

Pupil's pages 3 and 5

Acapulco Bay

Pupil's pages 6 and 7

Watch Your Step!

Pupil's page 8

Vigorous March

Les Ballons

Pupil's page 13

Gently and dreamily

Sleigh Ride
Pupil's page 23

Allegro Moderato

* N.B. These repeated bars are written out in full in the instrumental copy

Victorian Ballad

Pupil's page 26

* 2nd time to Coda

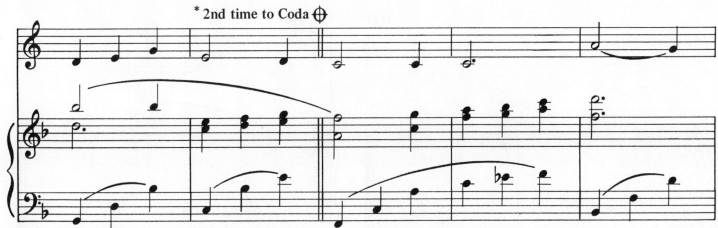

*The two-bar Coda appears only in the piano copy

My Favourite Things

Pupil's page 31

Words by OSCAR HAMMERSTEIN II
Music by RICHARD RODGERS

Edelweiss

Pupil's page 35

Words by OSCAR HAMMERSTEIN II
Music by RICHARD RODGERS

Theme from Polovtsian Dances

Pupil's page 36

ALEXANDER BORODIN (1833-87)

(Optional repeat mf)

Scottish Ballad

Pupil's page 43

Caribbean Dance
Pupil's page 44

The Centipede's Masterpiece

Pupil's page 58

SARAH HART

Printed by Halstan & Co. Ltd., Amersham, Bucks., England